STUDY GUIDE

RUN TO THE BROKENNESS

Copyright © 2025 by Kevin Foster

Published by AVAIL

All rights reserved. No portion of this book may be reproduced, stored in a retrieval system, or transmitted in any form or by any means—electronic, mechanical, photocopy, recording, scanning, or other—except for brief quotations in critical reviews or articles, without prior written permission of the author.

Unless otherwise specified, all Scripture quotations are taken from the Holy Bible, New International Version®, NIV®. Copyright © 1973, 1978, 1984, 2011 by Biblica, Inc.™ Used by permission of Zondervan. All rights reserved worldwide. www.zondervan.com. The "NIV" and "New International Version" are trademarks registered in the United States Patent and Trademark Office by Biblica, Inc.™ | Scripture quotations marked ESV are from The ESV® Bible (The Holy Bible, English Standard Version®), copyright © 2001 by Crossway, a publishing ministry of Good News Publishers. Used by permission. All rights reserved. | Scripture quotations marked NKJV are taken from the New King James Version®. Copyright © 1982 by Thomas Nelson. Used by permission. All rights reserved. | Scripture quotations marked NLT are taken from the Holy Bible, New Living Translation, copyright © 1996, 2004, 2015 by Tyndale House Foundation. Used by permission of Tyndale House Publishers, Inc., Carol Stream, Illinois 60188. All rights reserved.

For foreign and subsidiary rights, contact the author.

Cover design by: Sara Young
Cover photo by: Andrew van Tilborgh

ISBN: 978-1-964794-93-8   1 2 3 4 5 6 7 8 9 10

Printed in the United States of America

STUDY GUIDE

RUN TO THE BROKENNESS

KEVIN FOSTER

AVAIL

CONTENTS

INTRODUCTION 6

CHAPTER 1. **RETHINKING SUCCESS IN THE LOCAL CHURCH** 10

CHAPTER 2. **CHANGE THE METRICS** 16

CHAPTER 3. **IDENTIFY THE NEED** 22

CHAPTER 4. **RESPOND TO COMMUNITY CRISIS** 28

CHAPTER 5. **BROKENNESS IS AN OPPORTUNITY** 34

CHAPTER 6. **CREATING THE RIGHT CULTURE** 40

CHAPTER 7. **PASSION FOR YOUR COMMUNITY** 46

CHAPTER 8. **FUNDING THE MISSION** 52

CHAPTER 9. **OCCUPATIONAL HAZARDS OF MINISTRY** 58

CHAPTER 10. **YOU CAN CHANGE YOUR COMMUNITY** 64

RUN TO THE BROKENNESS

HOW YOUR CHURCH CAN BE THE CENTER OF YOUR COMMUNITY

KEVIN FOSTER

FOREWORD BY CHRIS SONKSEN

INTRODUCTION

Regardless of your Sunday attendance numbers, your church can become one of the most influential organizations in your city.

||| REVIEW, REFLECT, AND RESPOND |||

As you read the Introduction in *Run to the Brokenness*, review, reflect on, and respond to the text by answering the following questions.

How would you define what it means to "run to the brokenness," and how effectively is your church living that out right now?

_____
_____
_____
_____
_____
_____
_____
_____
_____

What metrics have you used to define success in ministry—and how have those metrics affected your motivation, sense of calling, or mental health?

_____
_____
_____
_____
_____
_____
_____
_____
_____
_____

When was the last time someone outside your church community came to you with a crisis—and what did that reveal about your church's perceived relevance?

_____
_____
_____
_____
_____
_____
_____
_____
_____
_____
_____
_____
_____

When have you felt like your vision was too impossible—and how does the author's story of starting with nothing challenge or encourage you?

_____
_____
_____
_____
_____
_____

What are you hoping to uncover about yourself and your church as you work through this study guide?

CHAPTER 1

RETHINKING SUCCESS IN THE LOCAL CHURCH

||| REVIEW, REFLECT, AND RESPOND |||

As you read Chapter 1: "Rethinking Success in the Local Church" in *Run to the Brokenness*, review, reflect on, and respond to the text by answering the following questions.

On a scale from 1 to 10, with 1 being "not at all" and 10 being "very well," how would you rate how effectively your church runs to the brokenness in your community—beyond the four walls of your building?

1   2   3   4   5   6   7   8   9   10

Where have you measured success by attendance, image, or approval instead of transformation?

_____
_____
_____
_____
_____
_____
_____
_____
_____
_____
_____
_____
_____
_____
_____

> *"And I tell you that you are Peter, and on this rock I will build my church, and the gates of Hades will not overcome it."*
>
> **—Matthew 16:18 (NIV)**

Consider the scripture above and answer the following questions:

When have you quietly carried the weight of "building the church" as if it were solely your responsibility? How has that pressure affected your joy, energy, or family?

_____
_____
_____
_____
_____
_____
_____
_____

How does this verse challenge the way you define success in ministry? What fears has that definition created—and how might those fears be limiting your church's reach, impact, and courage to run toward brokenness?

_____
_____
_____
_____
_____
_____
_____
_____

When have you prioritized Sunday gatherings over weekday impact? What needs to change?

_____
_____
_____
_____
_____
_____

What brokenness are you tempted to avoid because it's inconvenient, uncomfortable, or not "ministry as usual"?

_____
_____
_____
_____
_____
_____

What fears, assumptions, or attachments are keeping you from reimagining ministry beyond Sunday services—and how might those be limiting what God wants to do through you?

_____
_____
_____
_____
_____
_____

Who in your community is hungry, hurting, or overlooked—
and how might your church be uniquely positioned to respond?

_____
_____
_____
_____
_____
_____
_____
_____

When have you been discouraged by comparison in ministry?
How has that shaped your decisions, mindset, or sense
of calling?

_____
_____
_____
_____
_____
_____
_____
_____

What part of your leadership has been driven more by a fear of
decline than by faith in God's ability to rebuild?

_____
_____
_____

What stood out to you about the historical examples of churches serving as the center of civic, social, and spiritual life? How well is your church mirroring those examples?

What "successful" ministry models have you idolized—models that may look fruitful on the outside but have distracted you from the needs right outside your church doors?

CHAPTER 2

CHANGE THE METRICS

> **Success in the kingdom isn't about how many people sit in your seats—it's about how many lives you impact.**

||| REVIEW, REFLECT, AND RESPOND |||

As you read Chapter 2: "Change the Metrics" in *Run to the Brokenness*, review, reflect on, and respond to the text by answering the following questions.

What assumptions have you held about what "counts" in ministry that now need to be unlearned?

_____
_____
_____
_____

Your church may have strong discipleship systems—but are people being equipped to use their spiritual gifts to serve others, not just study more? Where is that missing?

_____
_____
_____
_____

Pastor Dishan Wickramaratne said, *"We have 1,000 pounds of teaching and only one ounce of practice,"* suggesting that congregations are often strong in information but lacking in true discipleship and real-world action. How do you feel about this statement? Is it true in your context? Is it true in the larger Body of Christ?

_____
_____
_____
_____

RUN TO THE BROKENNESS: STUDY GUIDE

> *"For I was hungry and you gave me something to eat,*
> *I was thirsty and you gave me something to drink,*
> *I was a stranger and you invited me in,*
> *I needed clothes and you clothed me,*
> *I was sick and you looked after me,*
> *I was in prison and you came to visit me."*
>
> **—Matthew 25:35-36 (NIV)**

Consider the scripture above and answer the following questions:

How closely do your church's current metrics reflect the values Jesus describes in this passage?

_____
_____
_____
_____
_____
_____

What would it require—financially, structurally, or emotionally—for your church to take this passage seriously as a blueprint for impact?

_____
_____
_____
_____
_____
_____
_____

Are you measuring how many people your church helps find employment, job training, or economic stability—or are those stories going unnoticed in your weekly metrics?

___

Think of someone like Jonathan, who experienced dignity and purpose through meaningful work. Does your church have any on-ramps for people like him—or are they left out of your ministry model?

___

During COVID-19, what new ministries or outreach efforts emerged—and why were some of those allowed to fade once Sunday returned?

___

What's one story from your church—like Amanda's or Maria's—that needs to be documented and celebrated as a key metric of transformation?

_____
_____
_____
_____
_____
_____

If someone audited your calendar, budget, and outreach strategy, what would they conclude your church is most committed to (i.e., social and economic impact or church growth maintenance)?

_____
_____
_____
_____
_____
_____

In what ways has your church become dependent on measuring success by what happens inside the sanctuary instead of what happens in the streets, stores, and homes of your community?

_____
_____
_____
_____

When have you hesitated to launch a practical outreach (like a food pantry, preschool, or job program) because it didn't feel "spiritual enough"? How might that mindset be limiting kingdom impact?

What internal resistance do you feel when you consider redefining success beyond traditional church metrics—and what fear, pride, or insecurity might be fueling that resistance?

CHAPTER 3

IDENTIFY THE NEED

 **IMPACT STARTS WITH PRESENCE. BUT PRESENCE STARTS WITH ASKING.**

||| REVIEW, REFLECT, AND RESPOND |||

As you read Chapter 3: "Identify the Need" in *Run to the Brokenness*, review, reflect on, and respond to the text by answering the following questions.

How might your Sunday-to-Sunday focus be limiting your church's potential for Monday-to-Saturday impact?

_____

_____

_____

_____

_____

_____

_____

_____

_____

When was the last time someone in your community asked your church for help? What does the frequency (or lack thereof) say about your presence in the neighborhood?

_____

_____

_____

_____

_____

_____

_____

_____

_____

> *"Give, and it will be given to you. A good measure, pressed down, shaken together and running over, will be poured into your lap."*
>
> **—Luke 6:38 (NIV)**

Consider the scripture above and answer the following questions:

What does it look like for your church to "give" beyond money—specifically in terms of presence, availability, and service to your community?

_____
_____
_____
_____
_____
_____
_____
_____

In what ways has a fear of scarcity or a scarcity mindset caused you to measure your outreach with caution instead of faith?

_____
_____
_____
_____
_____
_____
_____
_____

What local churches, businesses, schools, or government leaders are you currently collaborating with?

_____
_____
_____
_____
_____
_____

What barriers—internal or external—have kept you from partnering with them?

_____
_____
_____
_____
_____
_____

How are you actively building trust with schools, nonprofits, or civic leaders? What relationship needs to start this month?

_____
_____
_____
_____
_____
_____

If your church became known as a first responder to brokenness, what types of phone calls, partnerships, and opportunities would you need to prepare for?

_____
_____
_____
_____
_____
_____
_____
_____

What ideas about specific roles or gaps your church could fill in your own community did the crossing guard example spark?

_____
_____
_____
_____
_____
_____
_____
_____

Who could you invite to help you redefine and rework the way your church expands its reach—whether it's a trusted leader in your congregation or a partner from another church?

_____
_____
_____

When have you seen God's provision follow a simple, faithful yes? What is He asking you to say yes to now—and what's holding you back?

What in this chapter stirred something in you—and what specific action are you now compelled to take in your community as a result?

CHAPTER 4

RESPOND TO COMMUNITY CRISIS

 **The church should be the first to respond, not the last resort.**

||| REVIEW, REFLECT, AND RESPOND |||

As you read Chapter 4: "Respond to Community Crisis" in *Run to the Brokenness*, review, reflect on, and respond to the text by answering the following questions.

When tragedy hits your city, who do community leaders instinctively look to for help?

_____
_____
_____
_____
_____
_____
_____
_____
_____
_____

What held you back the last time you felt prompted to respond to a crisis—and what would you do differently now?

_____
_____
_____
_____
_____
_____
_____
_____
_____
_____

> *"This service that you perform is not only supplying the needs of the Lord's people but is also overflowing in many expressions of thanks to God."*
>
> **—2 Corinthians 9:12 (NIV)**

Consider the scripture above and answer the following questions:

How does your current level of service to the community demonstrate the gospel in a way that leads others to praise God—not just hear about Him?

_____
_____
_____
_____
_____
_____
_____
_____

What would need to change in your church's mindset, budget, or leadership structure to "prove yourselves" through radical service the next time a crisis hits?

_____
_____
_____
_____
_____
_____
_____
_____

How did the story of Cheryl and George challenge the way you measure transformation in your church? What if your church culture was the only gospel message someone like Cheryl would ever read?

_____
_____
_____
_____
_____
_____

Has your team been empowered to say yes when an urgent need arises—or are they stuck waiting for your permission? What process needs to shift?

_____
_____
_____
_____
_____
_____

What's one consistent pain point in your community that you've been aware of but haven't yet responded to with purpose?

_____
_____
_____
_____
_____
_____

Think about your church's physical space. How could it become a sanctuary of healing in the next crisis, not just a place for weekly services?

_____
_____
_____
_____
_____
_____
_____

What small act of presence—like curbside prayer or delivering lasagnas—could be your church's next act of obedience that leads to something bigger?

_____
_____
_____
_____
_____
_____
_____

If your church was awarded for being a "first responder" to spiritual and practical needs in your city, what would that award be recognizing? What are you doing now that deserves that recognition?

_____
_____
_____

If a crisis were to strike tomorrow, what internal system—volunteer mobilization, benevolence fund, communication chain—would fail first in your church, and why hasn't that been addressed yet?

What did this chapter expose about what your church is currently lacking when it comes to crisis response—and what root issue (fear, distraction, resource misalignment, apathy) is responsible for that gap?

CHAPTER 5

BROKENNESS IS AN OPPORTUNITY

 The church should be the first to respond, not the last resort.

||| REVIEW, REFLECT, AND RESPOND |||

As you read Chapter 5: "Brokenness Is an Opportunity" in *Run to the Brokenness*, review, reflect on, and respond to the text by answering the following questions.

Where in your city would people be shocked to see a pastor show up—and how might God be inviting you there?

_____
_____
_____
_____
_____
_____
_____
_____
_____

What struggles do you believe your congregation might be carrying?

_____
_____
_____
_____
_____
_____
_____
_____
_____

> "When Jesus came down from the mountainside, large crowds followed him. A man with leprosy came and knelt before him and said, 'Lord, if you are willing, you can make me clean.' Jesus reached out his hand and touched the man. 'I am willing,' he said. 'Be clean!' Immediately he was cleansed of his leprosy."
>
> **—Matthew 8:1-3 (NIV)**

Consider the scripture above and answer the following questions:

How is the pressure to play it safe or stay predictable keeping you from breaking the mold like Jesus did in this scripture?

_____
_____
_____
_____
_____
_____
_____

Think about the man with leprosy. Who in your community today resembles his experience of being avoided or cast aside—and what would it look like to draw near?

_____
_____
_____
_____
_____
_____
_____

Think back to the Egypt story. Has God ever whispered, "What if that someone is you?" into your spirit? How did you respond—and what might He be asking of you now?

_____
_____
_____
_____
_____
_____
_____

In what ways have you viewed brokenness as an obstacle rather than an opportunity?

_____
_____
_____
_____
_____
_____
_____

If you walked the streets of your city today with open eyes, what would you see differently? What do you feel called to respond to?

_____
_____
_____
_____
_____
_____
_____

In what ways have you unintentionally trained your church to prioritize order, comfort, or safety over proximity to pain?

_____
_____
_____
_____
_____
_____
_____
_____

The chapter says, "saying yes is the easy part." What commitment have you made to serve the broken that you haven't yet followed through on?

_____
_____
_____
_____
_____
_____
_____
_____

In your leadership, do you wait for brokenness to come to you, or are you actively looking for where it lives? What would it take to shift your posture?

_____
_____
_____

When you read about the woman who began praying at the strip club each week—despite not having a clear plan— what part of your ministry approach feels overplanned and under-prayed?

What insight, story, or challenge from this chapter struck you most—and why do you think it stood out to you?

CHAPTER 6

CREATING THE RIGHT CULTURE

 **God can plant you in a new environment and grow in you a different kind of fruit.**

||| REVIEW, REFLECT, AND RESPOND |||

**As you read Chapter 6: "Creating the Right Culture" in
Run to the Brokenness, review, reflect on, and respond
to the text by answering the following questions.**

What parts of your church's weekly rhythm feel effective but produce little lasting fruit in the lives of the hurting?

_____
_____
_____
_____
_____
_____
_____
_____

When was the last time you paused to ask: "Is this bearing good fruit—or just draining resources?"

_____
_____
_____
_____
_____
_____
_____
_____
_____
_____
_____

> *"A good tree produces good fruit, and a bad tree produces bad fruit . . . just as you can identify a tree by its fruit, you can identify people by their actions."*
>
> **—Matthew 7:17, 20 (NLT)**

Consider the scripture above and answer the following questions:

What fruit—tangible outcomes—has your church produced in the last year, and what does that reveal about your root system?

_____
_____
_____
_____
_____
_____
_____
_____
_____

If someone judged your ministry only by the lives changed outside the walls of your church, what would they conclude?

_____
_____
_____
_____
_____
_____
_____
_____
_____

If your church closed its doors tomorrow, what measurable fruit would remain in the lives of people in your community?

_____
_____
_____
_____
_____
_____

What kind of stories are you celebrating from the platform— and what do those stories reveal about your values?

_____
_____
_____
_____
_____
_____

What indicators do you currently use to measure fruitfulness? Which ones are helpful—and which ones might be distracting?

_____
_____
_____
_____
_____
_____
_____

RUN TO THE BROKENNESS: STUDY GUIDE

What would it look like to build a team culture that asks hard questions about fruit regularly without becoming critical or discouraged?

What have you tolerated in your ministry because it looks good on paper, even though it hasn't produced the kind of fruit God cares about?

What area of ministry do you instinctively avoid evaluating because you're afraid of what the fruit might reveal?

_____
_____
_____
_____
_____
_____
_____
_____
_____
_____

Who in your church is flourishing today because you prioritized depth over speed—and how can that become a model for future decisions?

_____
_____
_____
_____
_____
_____
_____
_____
_____
_____

CHAPTER 7

PASSION FOR YOUR COMMUNITY

> **GOD CAN PLANT YOU IN A NEW ENVIRONMENT AND GROW IN YOU A DIFFERENT KIND OF FRUIT.**

||| REVIEW, REFLECT, AND RESPOND |||

As you read Chapter 7: "Passion for Your Community" in *Run to the Brokenness*, **review, reflect on, and respond to the text by answering the following questions.**

What are the subtle signs that your church is picking up on your lack of passion for the community, even if you haven't said it out loud?

_____
_____
_____
_____
_____
_____
_____
_____
_____

If someone evaluated your week, how much time, energy, and prayer would they see going toward engaging the brokenness in your city?

_____
_____
_____
_____
_____
_____
_____
_____
_____

> *"Then I will give you shepherds after my own heart, who will lead you with knowledge and understanding."*
>
> **—Jeremiah 3:15 (NIV)**

Consider the scripture above and answer the following questions:

What does it mean for you, personally, to be a shepherd after God's own heart for your city—not just your church?

_____
_____
_____
_____
_____
_____
_____
_____

How well are you leading with knowledge and understanding when it comes to the specific brokenness of your city?

_____
_____
_____
_____
_____
_____
_____
_____

What personal resistance or disappointment has dulled your passion—either in the past or currently—for the place God planted you?

_____
_____
_____
_____
_____
_____
_____

The chapter says, "Passion is contagious." What have you unintentionally made contagious in your leadership—passion or passivity? Explain in detail.

_____
_____
_____
_____
_____
_____
_____

What does it practically look like for you to "dwell in the land" and "cultivate faithfulness" right where you are?

_____
_____
_____
_____
_____
_____
_____

What past comparisons or unmet expectations are still robbing you of joy and vision in your current assignment?

_____
_____
_____
_____
_____
_____
_____
_____

Think about your church's community reputation. Does it reflect the kind of consistent, visible investment that changes a city's perception? How do you know?

_____
_____
_____
_____
_____
_____
_____
_____

What vision has God given you that your people aren't ready for yet—and are you willing to carry it until they catch it?

_____
_____
_____

If your city grieves over something, do you grieve too—or have you become emotionally disconnected from its pain?

Have you been praying for your city by name—its leaders, schools, and neighborhoods—or have your prayers become confined to your church's needs? Why do you think this is?

CHAPTER 8

FUNDING THE MISSION

 **It's not just about revenue. It's about redemption.**

||| REVIEW, REFLECT, AND RESPOND |||

As you read Chapter 8: "Funding the Mission" in *Run to the Brokenness*, review, reflect on, and respond to the text by answering the following questions.

What limiting beliefs have you carried about church finances that keep you from reimagining funding in creative, God-honoring ways?

_____
_____
_____
_____
_____
_____
_____
_____

How would your budget—and your prayer life—change if you truly believed God wanted to fund your mission supernaturally?

_____
_____
_____
_____
_____
_____
_____
_____

> *"But if anyone has the world's goods and sees his brother in need, yet closes his heart against him, how does God's love abide in him?"*
>
> **—1 John 3:17 (ESV)**

Consider the scripture above and answer the following questions:

What "goods" has God already entrusted to you or your church that are currently going unused?

_____

_____

_____

_____

_____

_____

_____

What does failing to respond to need reveal about the presence—or absence—of God's love in us? What comes up for you as you consider this truth?

_____

_____

_____

_____

_____

_____

_____

What risks are you currently unwilling to take in faith, even though obedience might open the door to provision?

_____
_____
_____
_____
_____
_____

Who in your church has untapped gifts or business experience that could help your church build a sustainable income stream?

_____
_____
_____
_____
_____
_____

What would launching a social enterprise for your church and community require?

_____
_____
_____
_____
_____
_____

What objections have you used to delay launching a social enterprise or applying for grants—and are those objections grounded in fear or facts?

_____
_____
_____
_____
_____
_____
_____
_____

What types of jobs could your church realistically create that would both serve the community and disciple people through meaningful work?

_____
_____
_____
_____
_____
_____
_____
_____

What are you currently doing out of tradition that might be preventing you from discovering the new thing God wants to birth?

_____
_____

How are you helping new believers grow in generosity—and what's missing from your current discipleship pathway?

This chapter mentions how big change starts small. What's one small thing you can do this week to create long-lasting impact in your community?

CHAPTER 9

OCCUPATIONAL HAZARDS OF MINISTRY

 **MANY PASTORS DON'T REALIZE THE DANGER UNTIL IT'S TOO LATE.**

||| REVIEW, REFLECT, AND RESPOND |||

As you read Chapter 9: "Occupational Hazards of Ministry" in *Run to the Brokenness*, review, reflect on, and respond to the text by answering the following questions.

Which of the hazards in this chapter—emotional detachment, resentment, ego, insecurity, fatigue—have you seen grow in your life recently?

_____
_____
_____
_____
_____
_____
_____
_____
_____
_____

What are the subtle signs that you're tolerating or managing dysfunction rather than confronting it head-on?

_____
_____
_____
_____
_____
_____
_____
_____

 *"It is impossible that no offenses should come."*
—Luke 17:1 (NKJV)

Consider the scripture above and answer the following questions:

Jesus says offenses are inevitable. How have you prepared your heart and leadership for that reality—and where have you ignored it?

_____
_____
_____
_____
_____
_____
_____
_____

In what ways might you be unknowingly participating in someone else's offense or disillusionment with the church?

_____
_____
_____
_____
_____
_____
_____
_____

Where have you become numb in ministry, not because you don't care, but because caring too deeply has left you scarred?

_____
_____
_____
_____
_____
_____
_____

What decisions are you making right now that are shaped more by self-protection than by calling?

_____
_____
_____
_____
_____
_____
_____

How has insecurity affected the way you relate to other pastors or leaders in your region?

_____
_____
_____
_____
_____
_____

What conversations have you been avoiding with your team or family because you're afraid of being misunderstood or appearing weak?

_____
_____
_____
_____
_____
_____
_____

What boundaries have you failed to protect in the name of "ministry," and what has it cost you?

_____
_____
_____
_____
_____
_____
_____

Where are you placing your identity more in outcomes, influence, or comparison than in Christ?

_____
_____
_____

Where have you seen the cost of your insecurities, and how does Moses's fear about his ability to speak challenge the excuses you've made to shrink back from your calling?

What hazard in this chapter do you believe doesn't apply to you—and what would it look like to humbly revisit that assumption?

CHAPTER 10

YOU CAN CHANGE YOUR COMMUNITY

  God has more ways to fund His mission than we can imagine.

||| REVIEW, REFLECT, AND RESPOND |||

As you read Chapter 10: "You Can Change Your Community" in *Run to the Brokenness*, review, reflect on, and respond to the text by answering the following questions.

When have you felt most disqualified—and how has God met you in that moment?

What specific needs in your community have you noticed but ignored, believing someone else was better suited to respond?

> *"Do not consider his appearance or his height. . . . The LORD does not look at the things people look at. People look at the outward appearance, but the LORD looks at the heart."*
>
> **—1 Samuel 16:7 (NIV)**

Consider the scripture above and answer the following questions:

Where have you underestimated yourself—or your church—based on outward appearance, size, or resources?

_____
_____
_____
_____
_____
_____
_____
_____
_____

What would it look like to lead as someone whose qualifications rest solely on God's calling rather than human standards?

_____
_____
_____
_____
_____
_____
_____
_____
_____

When you consider the story of David being chosen over his more qualified brothers, what part of your own leadership journey does that mirror?

_____
_____
_____
_____
_____
_____
_____

What impact could your church make if you stopped focusing on your limitations and started asking God what's possible?

_____
_____
_____
_____
_____
_____
_____

What's one moment in your past that reminds you that God really did call you—and how might returning to that memory re-ignite your courage?

_____
_____
_____
_____
_____
_____
_____

Who in your congregation might be an "overlooked David"—called to lead, serve, or launch something new—but needs your encouragement?

_____
_____
_____
_____
_____
_____
_____

What's one dream or initiative you've buried because of a past failure, and what would it take to resurrect it?

_____
_____
_____
_____
_____
_____
_____

Write a personal prayer asking God to reveal what needs to change in you so you can more faithfully run to the brokenness in your community.

_____
_____
_____

If your ministry ended today, could you say with confidence that you fought for the right things, finished what God asked of you, and remained faithful even when it was hard?

What three things did this book reveal about you, your leadership, your church, and the needs of your community that were previously hidden or overlooked? How will you act on each of these discoveries?

www.ingramcontent.com/pod-product-compliance
Lightning Source LLC
Chambersburg PA
CBHW062122080426
42734CB00012B/2949